D1109846

The Works of
Christoph Nichelmann:
A Thematic Index

The Works of
Christoph Nichelmann:
A Thematic Index

by Douglas A. Lee

Detroit Studies in
Music Bibliography-19

Information Coordinators, Inc.
Detroit, 1971

Copyright 1971 by Douglas A. Lee
Printed and bound in the United States of America
Price $3.50
Library of Congress Catalog Card Number: 71-151301
Standard Book Number: 911772

INFORMATION COORDINATORS, INC
1435-37 Randolph Street
Detroit, Michigan 48226

TABLE OF CONTENTS

ACKNOWLEDGMENTS

It is a pleasure to acknowledge the assistance of individuals and institutions who have aided in the preparation of this index. I am particularly grateful to Dr. Karl-Heinz Köhler and the staff of the Deutsche Staatsbibliothek, Berlin, for invaluable help in gathering information on the location of many of the Nichelmann manuscripts; to Dr. Rolf Dempe, Mecklenburgische Landesbibliothek, Schwerin, for his assistance in obtaining copies of ensemble works; and to Dr. R. Münster, Bayerische Staatsbibliothek, Munich, for information relevant to Nichelmann's earliest published works. Other libraries have assisted by supplying microfilm copies of Nichelmann's works or have loaned valuable bibliographic material. These institutions include the Staatsbibliothek der Stiftung Preussischer Kulturbesitz, Musikabteilung, Berlin; the Sächsische Landesbibliothek, Dresden; the Universitätsbibliothek, Rostock; the Bibliothèque Nationale, Paris; and the British Museum, London.

INTRODUCTION

The continuing expansion of musicological research inherently regenerates itself. As the corpus of information expands it constantly raises new problems, opens new areas for study, and calls for new bibliographic tools to cope with these needs. A body of information which needs clarification relevant to the instrumental works of Christoph Nichelmann (b. 1717) is the location and correlation of manuscript sources surviving among German libraries. Robert Eitner's imposing Biographisch-bibliographisches Quellen-Lexikon[1] lists many of the manuscripts included here, but indications of autograph copies are incomplete, duplications receive no consideration, and many of the library collections to which he refers are no longer extant or have been incorporated into other institutions. Some works were destroyed during World

*   *   *

[1] Biographisch-bibliographisches Quellen-Lexikon der Musiker und Musikgelehrten der Christlichen Zeitrechnung bis zur Mitte des neunzehnten Jahrhunderts (11 vols.; reprint; New York: Musurgia, 1947), VII, 191-193.

War II, specifically, three trio sonatas in the Hessische Landes- und Hochschulbibliothek at Darmstadt. The Library of Princess Anna Amalia (1723-1787), sister of Friedrich the Great (1712-1786), contained many of Nichelmann's concerto manuscripts. This collection, the Amalienbibliothek, was assimilated into the library of the Joachimsthal Gymnasium prior to Eitner's work, but individual items retained their original catalogue numbers. Eitner gives no indication of this. The Joachimsthal Gymnasium was absorbed by the former Preussischen Staatsbibliothek in Berlin, later the Öffentliche Wissenschaftliche Bibliothek, now the Deutsche Staatsbibliothek, as a part of the Musikalien-sammlung Thulemeier. The situation was further complicated by the partial redistribution of this large collection during World War II. Some items came to rest in the Staatsbibliothek, Marburg/Lahn; some were returned to the present Deutsche Staatsbibliothek in Berlin; others have not yet been recovered. The Nichelmann manuscripts which were at Marburg/Lahn were returned to West Berlin in 1965 and are now contained within the Staatsbibliothek der Stiftung Preussischer Kulturbesitz. These items retain their original catalogue numbers and, in most instances, the earlier library stamp indicating their origins in the Joachimsthal Gymnasium and the Musikaliensammlung Thulemeier. The correlation of manuscripts for the index has uncovered three concertos of Nichelmann (Concertos I, II, III) which formerly had been catalogued in Berlin under the name Christoph Schaffrath (1719-1763). These works came to light with the revision and publication of the Amalienbibliothek catalogue in Eva (Bleckschmidt) Wutta's Die Amalien-Bibliothek: historische Einordnung und Katalog mit Hinweisen auf die Schreiben der Handschriften.[1] Wutta cites four such concerto manuscripts in full score, but one of these four is the original copy of a work previously known in part-book format in the Universitätsbibliothek Rostock (Concerto VIII).

Nichelmann's instrumental compositions fall

*   *   *

[1] (Berlin: Merseberger, 1965).

11

within three general traditions of instrumental music in the eighteenth century: concertos for a solo instrument and four-part string orchestra, sonatas and miscellaneous pieces for solo keyboard, and works for instrumental ensemble. His known compositions for voice include the serenata, Il sogno di Scipione (1746), a requiem calling for a four-part chorus and orchestra, a cantata for solo voice and strings, and songs for solo voice and keyboard variously titled Ode or Lied. The instrumental works far outnumber those for voice, they generally represent his better efforts, and many are important works relevant to the changing musical styles of the mid-eighteenth century. Most significant among these are the concertos. At a time when the accompanied keyboard concerto was relatively new, Nichelmann's works in this genre represent a well-formed structure presenting the keyboard in the role of a solo instrument with an established technique capable of an infinite variety of musical expression. The passagework given to the solo instrument reveals a healthy quality of physical exuberance through a technical freedom which stands well apart from the simple transfer of string passages to the keyboard. Among the works for solo keyboard, the sonatas alone constitute a significant body of literature. Many of the miscellaneous pieces can be described as musical miniatures, yet there are among them works which are outstanding in structure and musical vitality. The solo keyboard works enjoyed a wide circulation in the eighteenth century and are representative of much of the pre-classic keyboard literature.

DESCRIPTION OF SOURCES

The concertos are distributed in thirty manu-script copies, twelve of which are regarded as autograph sources. A number of factors distinguish the composer's manuscript from the work of copyists. Those manuscripts considered as autograph frequently contain sections which have been crossed out, altered, and sometimes extensively revised, changes which, on careful examination, clearly are the work of the composer. A signature which can only be presumed to be Nichelmann's own appears at the end of his Ouverture in B-flat. If the signature is Nichelmann's own hand, and there is no reason to think otherwise, that copy is representative of his musical calligraphy and can be identified readily with the twelve autograph sources listed in the index. Further, among the thirty manuscript copies of the concertos, the script of the twelve deemed autograph is much more consistent than the work of any other single scribe; the remaining eighteen copies show at least eight different styles of musical script. Taken together, these observations offer a reasonable support for the authenticity of the autographs.

No inference of chronology or progressive stylistic change is intended by the numbering of the concertos; they are listed according to the type and quantity of sources available for each. The numbering proceeds from works available in a single autograph to works represented by both autograph and copied versions, and concludes with works found in no autograph source.

The solitary violin concerto terminates the group. The first page of text in Concerto V is inscribed "1i 4 del mense / di Nov. 1743." Here Nichelmann probably is using the Italian "mense" in its ecclesiastical sense which refers to the altar. If so, "1i 4 del mense di Nov." would infer the liturgical Feast of the Four Crowned Martyrs (Sancti Quatuor Coronati), celebrated invariably on November 8. Thus, November 8, 1743, perhaps is the most logical and complete explanation of this inscription.[1] Of the two sources for Concerto IX, the manuscript score in Dresden differs from the autograph in some aspects of articulation and ornamentation. Like most of the scores in Dresden, this appears to have been prepared primarily for the keyboard performer. Frequently the string parts are only sketched out in the solo sections, while the keyboard part is written out in full. Eitner refers to five autograph

*   *   *

[1] See The Book of Saints, comp. Benedictine Monks of St. Augustine, Ramsgate (5th ed. rev.; New York: Thomas Y. Crowell Co., 1966), p. 282, and J. P. Kirsch, "Four Crowned Martyrs," The Catholic Encyclopedia, ed. C. G. Herbermann (15 vols.; New York: Robert Appleton Co., 1907-1912), VI, 163.

part-books for this concerto formerly catalogued as manuscript 168 in the Musikaliensammlung Thulemeier in Berlin.[1] This collection is now a part of the Deutsche Staatsbibliothek, but the part-books for Concerto IX have been lost. The work was also included in Part Four of "Catalogo dei soli, duetti, trii, terzetti, quartetti e concerti per il cembalo e l'harpa che si trovano in manoscritto nella officina musica di Breitkopf," 1763.[2] Source B for Concerto X apparently was copied by two different scribes and is inaccurate in that all parts do not contain the same number of measures in the first movement. Of the four copies of Concerto XI, no two were copied by the same hand. The autograph score lacks the end of the third movement, but the missing sixteen measures are complete in the other sources. An autograph keyboard part for this concerto in the Hessische Landes- und Hochschulbibliothek at Darmstadt

*   *   *

[1] Thematischer Katalog von der Thulemeierschen Musikaliensammlung in der Bibliothek des Joachimsthalschen Gymnasium zu Berlin (Leipzig: Breitkopf & Hartel, 1899), p. 72.

[2] See Barry S. Brook, ed., The Breitkopf Thematic Catalogue; the Six Parts and Sixteen Supplements (New York: Dover Publications, 1966), p. 134.

was destroyed during World War II. Concerto XIV is a quite different version of Concerto VII. The only elements held in common are the basic tonic and a similarity of head-motives in corresponding movements. The part-books comprising source B are bound in a very confused order; on the title pages of sources A and C the name of Emanuel Bach (1714-1788) has been added in a strange hand, but the concerto was not included in Wotquenne's catalogue of Bach's works. Other studies have confused this work with Concerto VII, but a careful comparison of the part-books listed above definitely ascertains they are the same, and that these three sources represent a work independent from that listed as Concerto VII. It is worth noting that Concertos XV and XVI were both arranged for two keyboards, a practice relatively common in the eighteenth century as it is now, and one which may attest to a degree of popularity for these works.

The numbering of the sonatas is based on their early prominence and distribution by groups. Sonatas I through VI first appeared as Sei brevi Sonate / da

Cembalo / massime all' uso delle Dame / D. D. D.

Alla Sacra e Real Maesta / Federico II / Re de Prussia,

published at Nürnberg by Balthasar Schmid (1705-1749

August 30, 1745.[2] The erroneous publication date

1749 was first ascribed to this set by Fétis[3] and ha

been repeated without question by subsequent writers

Schmid published from 1726 until his death in 1749

His widow continued until 1786, but works publishe

under her direction are designated "Balth. Schmi

seel. Wittib." So the title page alone casts doubt o

the date given by Fétis. Schmid also published

second set of six sonatas (VIII-XIII) with a title pag

quite similar to the first and the catalogue numbe

XXVI. According to the Musikverlags Nummern c

*   *   *

[1] Six Short Sonatas for the Harpsichord, Chiefly for the use of t
Ladies; To his Sacred and Royal Majesty, Friedrich II, King of Prussi
The initials D. D. D. may be individuals for whom Nichelmann actual
intended the sonatas. The same initials appeared on the first set of s
sonatas by Emanuel Bach, published by Schmid in 1742, so they possib
were an ascription of the publisher. The thematic catalogue of Bach
works offers no explanation for the initials.

[2] Horst Heussner, "Der Musikdrucker Balthasar Schmid in Nürnberg
Die Musikforschung, XVI (October, 1963), 356, and Otto Eric Deutsc
Musikverlags Nummern (Berlin: Merseburger, 1961), pp. 22-23.

[3] Francois-Joseph Fétis, Biographie universelle des musicie
(8 vols.; 2nd ed.; Paris: Firmin-Didot, 1877-1878), VI, 311.

Sei brevi Sonate

da Cembalo

massime all'uso delle Dame

D. D. D.

Alla Sacra e Real Maestà

FEDERICO II.

Rè de Prussia

da

Cristoforo Nichelmann.

alle Spese di Balth. Schmid Norimberg

N.° XXIV.

)eutsch, the number XXVI in Schmid's publications
ould have appeared sometime during 1744 or 1745.
n his listing of Schmid's catalogue, Heussner gives
he date 1748, obtained from a catalogue of music
ublications compiled by Johann Jakob Lotter (1726-
804).[1] The publication of both sets may have been
onnected with Nichelmann's appointment to the royal
hapel of Friedrich the Great. Sonatas XV through
VIII are sonatas three, four, five, and six of an
riginal manuscript collection of six; there is no clear
ecord of the sonatas that were originally the first two
f the group. However, the fourth part of the thematic
atalogue issued by Breitkopf in 1763 included the
icipits of two sonatas by Nichelmann.[2] The first is
onata XIV of this index. Concerning the second, in
minor, no further information is available but it may
e these two manuscript works listed by Breitkopf were
iginally a part of the manuscript collection

*   *   *

[1] Catalogus aller musikalischen Bücher, Augsberg, 1753.
[2] See the facsimile in Brook, The Breitkopf Thematic Catalogue,
120.

mentioned above.

Source entries within the index supply all relevant information for the remaining works.

BIOGRAPHICAL SKETCH

The first biographical account of Christoph Nichelmann appeared in F. W. Marpurg's Historisch krittische Beyträge under the subheading "Lebensläuff verschiedenen lebenden Tonkünstler."[1] This articl served as the basis for many subsequent biographies i the eighteenth and nineteenth centuries. A more recer study by Heinz Döllmann, Christoph Nichelmann, ei Musiker am Hofe Friedrichs des Grossen,[2] repea Marpurg verbatim, and the article in Die Musik i Geschichte und Gegenwart derives directly from th

*　　*　　*

[1]Friedrich Wilhelm Marpurg, Historisch-krittische Beyträge z Aufnahme der Musik (5 vols.; Berlin: Schütz (I) and G. A. Lang (II-V 1754-1778), I, 431-439.
[2](Löningen: Friedrich Schmücker, 1938).

20

llman work.[1] The sketch of Nichelmann's life

cluded here presents the essential information from

arpurg's article with some supplementary data.

Nichelmann was born August 13, 1717, at

euenbrietzen, some forty miles south and west of

rlin. His early musical progress in keyboard playing

d in singing was such that in 1730 he was sent to the

iomasschule in Leipzig for more formal instruction

om the famous cantor, Johann Sebastian Bach. There

no evidence that Nichelmann received any private

struction from Sebastian Bach other than that

ceived by all boys at the school. Nichelmann did

ceive private lessons in keyboard playing from

ilhelm Friedemann Bach (1710-1784), however, and

was under Friedemann's direction that he made his

rst attempts at composition.

Within the environs of Leipzig and the Thomas-

*   *   *

[1] Thomas-Martin Langner, "Nichelmann," Die Musik in Geschichte
d Gegenwart, ed. Friedrich Blume (14 vols.; Kassel: Bärenreiter, 1949-
68), IX, 1441-1443. For a more extensive bio-bibliographical study of
chelmann, see this author's The Instrumental Works of Christoph
chelmann (2 vols.; Ann Arbor: University Microfilms, 1968).

schule, Nichelmann surely would have heard much o
Sebastian Bach's instrumental music, for solos a
concertos on various instruments were frequently playe
during the church service. Among Bach's keyboar
concertos deriving from this period are those in D mino
and E major (BWV 1052 and 1053); Nichelmann certainl
knew the E-major concerto, for at some time he copie
out the parts, perhaps for performance or for his ow
study. The work appears in the index followin
Nichelmann's own authenticated concertos.

After three years at Leipzig, Nichelmann began
series of travels which were to occupy him for the nex
twelve years. In 1733 he travelled to Hamburg for th
express purpose of becoming more closely acquainte
with opera. He evidently had a capacity for makin
his way rapidly, for he obtained instruction from th
three reigning musicians of that city, Reinhard Keise
(1674-1739), George Philipp Telemann (1681-1767)
and Johann Mattheson (1681-1764). Nichelmann late
continued his studies in Berlin with Johann Joachi
Quantz (1697-1773) and Carl Heinrich Graun (1704

1759), both members of the noted musical establishment created by Friedrich the Great. Nichelmann's first published keyboard works stem from this period, and in 1745 he joined Carl Philipp Emanuel Bach as one of two keyboardists in the royal chapel of Friedrich II. Biographers consistently have described Nichelmann as a second keyboardist at court, but this is open to question. No account mentions Nichelmann in a subordinate role at the keyboard, whereas several do refer to his good standing in the king's esteem in the domain of opera. Statements by nineteenth- and twentieth-century biographers that Nichelmann occupied a position secondary to that of Emanuel Bach are assumptions based on Bach's later renown.

Nichelmann wrote both instrumental and vocal works while in the service of the king, but a work which received more attention from his contemporaries was an extended theoretical treatise, Die Melodie nach ihrem Wesen sowohl, als nach ihren Eigenschaften. [1]

*   *   *

[1](Danzig: J. C. Schuster, and Hamburg: C. Herold, 1755).

The work elicited some sharp literary criticism from a pseudonymous Caspar Dünkelfeind in Gedanken eines Liebhabers der Tonkunst über Herrn Nichelmanns Tractat von der Melodie,[1] criticism answered in the fashion of the time by Nichelmann in Die Vortrefflich-keit der Gedanken des Herrn Caspar Dünkelfeindes über die Abhandlung von der Melodie ins Licht gesetzt von einem Musick Freunde.[2] Circumstantial evidence suggests Dünkelfeind may have been a pen name for Emanuel Bach.[3] Nichelmann left the court in 1756, by his own volition, according to Marpurg, but remained in the vicinity of Berlin and moved in the group of personalities later known as the Berlin Liederkreis.

The upheaval of the Seven Years' War perhaps was responsible for lack of definitive information on Nichelmann's death. The first report, in Gerber, puts

*   *   *

[1] (Nordhausen: July 1, 1755).
[2] No place or date of publication given.
[3] See the discussion in The Instrumental Works of Christoph Nichelmann, I, 39-46.

"around 1761."[1] The first specific date appeared

1861 in Ledebur's <u>Tonkünstler-Lexikon Berlins</u>,

here it is given as July 20, 1762.[2] Ledebur does not

isclose the source of his information, but it is

mpting to accept such a definite date when confronted

ith the uncertainty of the others. Until more

formation is available, the date 1761/1762 probably

the most honest that can be given for Nichelmann's

eath.

*   *   *

---

[1] Ernst Ludwig Gerber, <u>Historische-biographisches Lexicon der onkünstler</u> (2 vols.; Leipzig: Breitkopf, 1790-1792), II, 27.

[2] Carl F. Ledebur, <u>Tonkünstler-Lexikon Berlins</u> (Berlin: Ludwig auh, 1861), p. 394.

CONCERTOS FOR KEYBOARD AND STRINGS

CONCERTOS FOR KEYBOARD AND STRINGS

ONCERTO I

llegro, 118 measures

dagio, 153 measures

llegretto, 227 measures

A. "Concerto / per il Cembalo / con due Violini / 1 Viola /
e Continuo / da CN.," December 8, 1740.
Berlin: Deutsche Staatsbibliothek, Ab. 586, score and
five part-books (autograph).

ONCERTO II

llegro, 209 measures

CONCERTO II (Continued)

Adagio, 60 measures

Allegro, 183 measures

    A.   "Concerto / a / Cembalo Concertato / Violino 1mo /
        Violino 2do / Viola / e / Basso."
        Berlin: Deutsche Staatsbibliothek, Ab. 587, score
        (autograph).

Another slow movement, Largo, is included in the manuscript but has
been crossed out and replaced by the slow movement given above.

Largo, 64 measures

CONCERTO III

Allegrissimo, 199 measures

ndante, 77 measures

ivace, 244 measures

A. "Concerto / a Cembalo Concertato, due Violini / Viola
e Basso," January 30, 1758.
Berlin: Deutsche Staatsbibliothek, Ab. 588, score
(autograph).

ONCERTO IV

pirituoso, 248 measures

dagio, 91 measures

llegro, 297 measures

A. "Concert per il Cembal: concert. / del Sig^re / Nichelman /
A dur."
Berlin: Deutsche Staatsbibliothek, Ab. 517, score
(autograph).

CONCERTO V

Allegro, 248 measures

Adagio, 86 measures

Presto, 290 measures

A. "Concerto / Cembalo Concertato / Violino Primo / Violino
Secondo / Viola et / Basso / Dell Sig / Nichelmann,"
November, 1743.
Berlin: Deutsche Staatsbibliothek, Ab. 520, score
(autograph).

CONCERTO VI

Allegro, 259 measures

Adagio, 70 measures

Presto, 254 measures

A.   "Concerto C moll / Clavicembalo concertanto / Violino
     primo / Violino secondo / Viola / et / Basso / Sign.
     Nichelmann."
     Berlin: Deutsche Staatsbibliothek, M. Th. 169, five
     part-books (autograph).

CONCERTO VII

Allegro, 271 measures

Adagio, 38 measures

Presto, 209 measures

A.   "Concerto D moll / per il Cembalo concert. / Violino
     primo / Violino secondo / Viola e / Basso / di Nichelmann.
     1759," August 17, 1759.
     Berlin: Deutsche Staatsbibliothek, M. Th. 170, score
     (autograph) and four part-books.

CONCERTO VIII

Moderato, 107 measures

Adagio, 52 measures

Allegro, 197 measures

A. "Concerto / a Cembalo, due Violini, Viola / e Basso."
Berlin: Deutsche Staatsbibliothek, Ab. 591, score
(autograph). The last page of the Allegro is missing.

B. "Concerto. / A 5. / Cembalo Concerto. / Violino Primo.
/ Violino Secondo / Viola / et / Basso / del Sig.
Nichelmann."
Rostock: Universitätsbibliothek Rostock, Mus. saec.
XVIII, 49^2, five part-books.

CONCERTO IX

Allegretto, 170 measures

ndante, 71 measures

resto, 290 measures

A. "Concerto per il Cemb. concert: / del Sig / Nichelman /
    C dur," September 8, 1751.
    Berlin: Deutsche Staatsbibliothek, Ab. 519, score
    (autograph).

B. "Concerto per il Cembalo di Nichelman (C dur)."
    Dresden: Sächsische Landesbibliothek, Mus. MS
    3051/0/4, score.

ONCERTO X

oderato, 132 measures

dagio, 39 measures

CONCERTO X (Continued)

Allegro, 232 measures

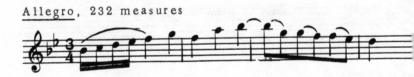

A. "Concerto / per Cembalo / di Nichelmann."
   Berlin: Deutsche Staatsbibliothek, Ab. 521, score
   (autograph).

B. "Concerto in B / per il / Clavicembalo / concertanto /
   Violino Primo / Violino Secondo / Viola e / Basso Ripieno."
   Berlin: Staatsbibliothek der Stiftung Preussischer Kul-
   turbesitz, Mus. MS 16165/7, five part-books.

CONCERTO XI

Allegro, 179 measures

Andantino, 56 measures

Vivace, 300 measures

A. "Concerto del S. Nichelman / per il Cembalo concertato.
    / C dur."
    Berlin: Deutsche Staatsbibliothek, Ab. 522, score
    (autograph).

B. "Concerto C♯/ per il Cembalo / dal Sgr Nichelmann."
    Berlin: Staatsbibliothek der Stiftung Preussischer
    Kulturbesitz, Mus. MS 16165/5, five part-books.

C. "Concerto per il Cembalo di Nichelman (C dur)."
    Dresden: Sächsische Landesbibliothek, Mus. MS
    3051/0/3, score.

D. "Concerto a 5 / per il Cembalo. / dal Sig. / Nichelmann."
    Brussels: Bibliothèque du Conservatoire royal de
    musique, Litt. 6154(2), five part-books.

CERTO XII

egro, 134 measures

agio, 37 measures

ace, 168 measures

A. "Concerto per il Cembalo di Nichelman (Es dur)."
    Dresden: Sächsische Landesbibliothek, Mus. MS
    3051/0/5, score.

CONCERTO XIII

Un Poco Allegro, 77 measures

Largo, 61 measures

Presto, 229 measures

A. "Concerto / da Sigr. Nichelmann."
Berlin: Staatsbibliothek der Stiftung Preussischer
Kulturbesitz, Mus. MS 16165/3, five part-books.

CONCERTO XIV

Allegro, 231 measures

Adagio, 87 measures

Allegro, 212 measures

A. "D moll / Concerto a Cembalo / Concertato / Violino
Primo / Violino Secondo / Viola / & / Basso / del /
Sigr. C. F. E. Bach."
Berlin: Staatsbibliothek der Stiftung Preussischer
Kulturbesitz, Mus. MS Bach 926, five part-books.

B. "Concerto / D moll / per il Cembalo concertato /
accompagnato / da due Violini, Violetta e Basso /
dal Sigr. Nichelmann."
Brussels: Bibliothèque du Conservatoire royal de
musique, Litt. 6154(3), five part-books.

C. "d moll / Concerto. / Cembalo Concertato / Violino
1mo. / Violino 2do. / Viola. / Basso / di / C. P. E.
Bach."
Vienna: Gesellschaft der Musikfreunde in Wien,
Mus. MS VII 36258, five part-books.

CONCERTO XV

Allegro, 228 measures

Adagio, 87 measures

CONCERTO XV (Continued)

Presto, 292 measures

A. "Concerto di Cembalo / accompagnato / da / Due
Violini, Viole, e Violoncello / di / Signore Nichelmann."
Berlin: Staatsbibliothek der Stiftung Preussischer
Kulturbesitz, Mus. MS 16165/1, five part-books.

B. "Concerto per il Cembalo / con / due Violini, Viola,
e Basso / di Nichelman (F dur)."
Dresden: Sächsische Landesbibliothek, Mus. MS
3051/0/1, five part-books.

C. "Concerto / a / Due Cembali / di Nichelmann."
Dresden: Sächsische Landesbibliothek, Mus. MS
3051/0/6, two part-books for first and second keyboards.

D. "Concerto / per il / Cembalo / due Violini / Viola. /
et / Basso / del Sig. Nichelman."
Rostock: Universitätsbibliothek Rostock, Mus. saec.
XVIII 49^{3a}, five part-books.

CONCERTO XVI

Allegro, 187 measures

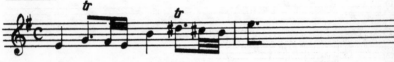

Largo, 98 measures

Vivace, 379 measures

A. "Concerto per il Cembalo / con due Violini, Viola, e
Basso / del Sig^re Nichelman (E moll)."
Dresden: Sächsische Landesbibliothek, Mus. MS
3051/0/2, eight part-books.

B. "Concerto / a / Due Cembali / di Nichelmann."
Dresden: Sächsische Landesbibliothek, Mus. MS
3051/0/6, two part-books for first and second keyboards.

C. "Concerto a 5 / per il Cembalo / del Seg. / Nichelmann."
Brussels: Bibliothèque du Conservatoire royal de
musique, Litt. 6154(1), five part-books.

CONCERTO XVII (violin concerto)

Tempo lacking, 161 measures

Adagio, 60 measures

Allegro, 215 measures

A. "Concerto per il Cembalo conc: / A# / del Sig^re Nichelman."
Berlin: Deutsche Staatsbibliothek, Ab. 518, score
(autograph).

CONCERTO IN E MAJOR

Tempo lacking, 175 measures

Siciliano, 37 measures

Allegro, 395 measures

A. "Concerto / per / Cembalo Concertato del Sign.
Nichelmann / con / Violino primo / Violino secondo /
Viola / e / Basso."
Berlin: Deutsche Staatsbibliothek, M. Th. 270,
score and four part-books (autograph).

The concerto is identical with the Sebastian Bach concerto in
E-major, BWV 1053, and obviously is a spurious attribution
to Nichelmann. See Johann Sebastian Bach's Werke, ed.
Bach-Gesellschaft zu Leipzig (46 vols.; reprint of Breitkopf &
Hartel ed.; Ann Arbor: Edwards Bros., 1947), XVII, 45-78.

SONATAS FOR SOLO KEYBOARD

SONATAS FOR SOLO KEYBOARD

SONATA I

Moderato, 31 measures

Largo, 47 measures

Vivace, 64 measures

A. "Sonata ex G moll," Moderato only.
   Berlin: Staatsbibliothek der Stiftung Preussischer
   Kulturbesitz, Mus. MS 30431.

B. "VI Sonate / per il Cembalo / da Nichelmann," no. 1.
   Brussels: Bibliothèque du Conservatoire royal de
   musique, Litt. 6153.

C. Sei brevi Sonate / da Cembalo / massime all' uso delle
   Dame / D. D. D. / Alla Sacra e Real Maesta / Federico
   II / Re de Prussia, no. 1.
   Nürnberg: Balthasar Schmid, 1745.

Neither manuscript copy is Nichelmann's autograph.
Source B was apparently copied from the printed edition.

SONATA II

Allegretto, 91 measures

Mesto, 15 measures

Presto, 77 measures

A. "VI Sonate," no. 2.
    Brussels: Bibliothèque du Conservatoire royal de
    musique, Litt. 6153.

B. Sei brevi Sonate, no. 2.
    Nürnberg: B. Schmid, 1745.

SONATA III

Un poco Allegro, 45 measures

Andantino, 32 measures

Presto, 116 measures

A. "VI Sonate," no. 3.
   Brussels: Bibliothèque du Conservatoire royal de musique, Litt. 6153.

B. Sei brevi Sonate, no. 2.
   Nürnberg: B. Schmid, 1745.

SONATA IV

Allegretto, 89 measures

Largo, 32 measures

Vivace, 58 measures

A. "VI Sonate," no. 4.
   Brussels: Bibliothèque du Conservatoire royal de musique, Litt. 6153.

B. "Sonate / per Cembalo."
   Berlin: Staatsbibliothek der Stiftung Preussischer Kulturbesitz, Mus. MS 16166.

C. Sei brevi Sonate, no. 4.
   Nürnberg: B. Schmid, 1745.

SONATA V

Un poco Allegro, 46 measures

Andante, 38 measures

Presto, 117 measures

A. "VI Sonate," no. 5.
   Brussels: Bibliothèque du Conservatoire royal de
   musique, Litt. 6153.

B. Sei brevi Sonate, no. 5.
   Nürnberg: B. Schmid, 1745.

SONATA VI

Allegro, 93 measures

Adagio, 20 measures

resto, 163 measures

A. Sei brevi Sonate, no. 6.
   Nürnberg: B. Schmid, 1745.

ONATA VII

empo lacking, 93 measures

empo lacking, 19 measures

empo lacking, "Divert Allegro ex F," incomplete after measure 24

A. "Clavier / Buch / pro / 1773."
   Berlin: Staatsbibliothek der Stiftung Preussischer
   Kulturbesitz, Mus. MS 30433, pp. 10-12.

The first movement is quite similar to that of Sonata VI, but
the second and third movements are obviously spurious. The
entire manuscript was copied in a hand other than Nichelmann's.

SONATA VIII

Allegretto, 82 measures

Largo, 37 measures

Presto, 48 measures

A. Brevi Sonate / da Cembalo / all' uso di chi ama il
    Cembalo / massime delle Dame / da / Cristofforo
    Nichelmann / nel Servizio di S. M. / il Re di Prussia /
    Opera IIda, no. 1.
    Nürnberg: Balthasar Schmid, ca. 1745.

B. Six / Short Sonatas or Lessons / for the / HARPSICHORD /
    Design'd for the Improvement of all Lovers of that
    Instrument and Chiefly for the / Ladies, by / Cristofforo
    Nichelman, no. 1.
    London: Longman, Lukey & Co., ca. 1770.

SONATA IX

Un poco Allegro, 55 measures

ndante, 26 measures

resto, 117 measures

    A. Brevi Sonate, no. 2.
       Nürnberg: B. Schmid, ca. 1745.

    B. Six Short Sonatas, no. 2.
       London: Longman, Lukey & Co., ca. 1770

ONATA X

llegro, 56 measures

argo, 31 measures

llegretto, 60 measures

    A. Brevi Sonate, no. 3.
       Nürnberg: B. Schmid, ca. 1745

    B. Six Short Sonatas, no. 3.
       London: Longman, Lukey & Co., ca. 1770

SONATA XI

Allegro, 57 measures

Adagio, 18 measures

Allegro, 104 measures

     A.   Brevi Sonate, no. 4.
           Nürnberg: B. Schmid, ca. 1745.

     B.   Six Short Sonatas, no. 4.
           London: Longman, Lukey & Co., ca. 1770

SONATA XII

Allegro, 34 measures

Andante, 29 measures

llegro, 54 measures

A. Brevi Sonate, no. 5.
   Nürnberg: B. Schmid, ca. 1745.

B. Six Short Sonatas, no. 5.
   London: Longman, Lukey & Co., ca. 1770.

ONATA XIII

llegro, 80 measures

ndante, 20 measures

esto, 105 measures

A. Brevi Sonate, no. 6.
   Nürnberg: B. Schmid, ca. 1745.

B. Six Short Sonatas, no. 6.
   London: Longman, Lukey & Co., ca. 1770.

SONATA XIV

Allegro, 101 measures

Larghetto, 100 measures

Vivace, 60 measures

    A. "Sonata per il Cembalo," November 13, 1741.
       Paris: Bibliothèque nationale, Mus. MS 2144
       (autograph).

SONATA XV

Allegro, 73 measures

Larghetto, 103 measures

Vivace, 60 measures

A. "VI Sonate / da Cembalo / di Nichelmann," no. 3.
Berlin: Deutsche Staatsbibliothek, M. Th. 173
(autograph).

Sonatas one and two of this collection are missing. The
above work is apparently a later version of Sonata XIV.

SONATA XVI

Allegro, 82 measures

Andante, 21 measures

Allegro, 100 measures

A. "VI Sonate / da Cembalo," no. 4.
Berlin: Deutsche Staatsbibliothek, M. Th. 173
(autograph).

This autograph copy is followed in the manuscript
collection by a very rough sketch of the first movement
which may have been Nichelmann's original draft.

SONATA XVII

Allegro moderato, 64 measures

Largo, 17 measures

Presto, 94 measures

A. "VI Sonate / da Cembalo," no. 5.
    Berlin: Deutsche Staatsbibliothek, M. Th. 173
    (autograph).

SONATA XVIII

Allegro, 90 measures

Andante, 50 measures

Presto, 103 measures

A. "VI Sonate / da Cembalo," no. 6.
Berlin: Deutsche Staatsbibliothek, M. Th. 173
(autograph).

SONATA XIX

Allegro, 59 measures

Andante, 20 measures

Allegretto, 58 measures

A. "Sonate von Nichelmann."
Berlin: Deutsche Staatsbibliothek, Mus. MS 103.

B. "Klavier und Kirchenmusik / von / Bach, Guilain, Händel,
Just, u. a."
Berlin: Deutsche Staatsbibliothek, Mus. MS 30819, pp. 5-8.

C. Tonstücke für das Clavier / von / Herrn C. P. E. Bach und
einiges andern classischen Musikern.
Berlin: Arnold Wever, 1774, pp. 16-22.

SONATA XIX (Continued)

D. C. P. E. Bachs, Nichelmanns und Händels / Sonaten und Fugen / fürs Clavier. 2nd ed. Berlin: Arnold Wever, 1774, pp. 16-22.

Sonata XIX is apparently a later version of Sonata XVI. Similarity of articulation and pagination indicate manuscript version A was copied from one of the printed editions.

SONATA XX

Vivace, 36 measures

Andante alla Polacca, 18 measures

Allegro non molto, 61 measures

A. "Sonatina / per il / Cembalo. / di Nichelman." Rostock: Universitätsbibliothek, Mus. saec. XVIII 49[1] (autograph).

SONATA IN C MINOR

Allegro, 74 measures

Adagio, 41 measures

Allegro, 218 measures

A. "VI Sonate," no. 6.
    Brussels: Bibliothèque du Conservatoire royal de
    musique, Litt. 6153.

The sonata is falsely attributed to Nichelmann in the above source.
It is identical with a "Clavicembalo Solo / dell' Sig. / Graun."
Dresden: Sächsische Landesbibliothek, Mus. MS 2953/T/1.

MISCELLANEOUS WORKS FOR SOLO KEYBOARD

MISCELLANEOUS WORKS FOR SOLO KEYBOARD

<u>Allegro</u>, 96 measures

A. Berlin: Staatsbibliothek der Stiftung Preussischer
Kulturbesitz, Mus. MS Bach P. 366, pp. 30-31.

B. "Sonate."
Berlin: Staatsbibliothek der Stiftung Preussischer
Kulturbesitz, Mus. MS Bach P. 295, pp. 100-102.

C. Raccolta / delle / piu nuove composizioni / di
clavicembalo / di differenti maestri ed autori.
Ed. Friedrich W. Marpurg. Two volumes.
Leipzig: Gio. Gottl. Iman. Breitkopf, 1756-1757,
I, 40-41.

<u>Allegro</u>, 48 measures

A. Berlin: Deutsche Staatsbibliothek, Mus. MS 30201.

B. Raccolta / delle / piu nuove composizioni / di
clavicembalo / di differenti maestri ed autori.
Ed. Friedrich W. Marpurg. Two volumes.
Leipzig: Gio. Gottl. Iman. Breitkopf, 1756-1757,
II, 9-10.

<u>Allegro</u>, 49 measures

A. Musikalisches Allerley / von / verschiedenen Tonkünstlern.
Nine volumes.
Berlin: F. W. Birnstiel, 1761-1763, VI, 177-178.

Allegretto, 64 measures

A. "Sonate," Clavierstücke / mit einem practischen Unterricht / für Anfänger und Geübtere. Ed. Friedrich W. Marpurg. Three volumes.
Berlin: Haude & Spener, 1762-1763, I, Tab. VIII.

Allegro, 92 measures

A. "Sonate," Clavierstücke / mit einem practischen Unterricht / für Anfänger und Geübtere. Ed. Friedrich W. Marpurg. Three volumes.
Berlin: Haude & Spener, 1762-1763, II, 10-12.

Prestо́, 137 measures

A. Clavierstücke / mit einem practischen Unterricht / für Anfänger und Geübtere. Ed. Friedrich W. Marpurg. Three volumes.
Berlin: Haude & Spener, 1762-1763, III, 6-9.

LA GAILLARDE AND LA TENDRE

La Gaillarde, 44 measures

a Tendre, 36 measures

A. Musikalisches Allerley von verschiedenen Tonkünstlern.
Nine volumes.
Berlin: F. W. Birnstiel, 1761-1763, I, 29-30.

_AVIERSUITE

llegro, 16 measures

arabande: Adagio, 16 measures

igue: Presto, 30 measures

A. Musikalisches Allerley von verschiedenen Tonkünstlern.
Nine volumes.
Berlin: F. W. Birnstiel, 1761-1763, V, 121, 125-126.

X MENUETS

measures

SIX MENUETS (Continued)

24 measures

16 measures

32 measures

24 measures

24 measures

A. Berlin: Deutsche Staatsbibliothek, Mus. MS 103
(autograph).

This collection of Nichelmann's manuscripts
has also been designated as Nichelmann 1 N.

IX POLONAISES

6 measures

4 measures

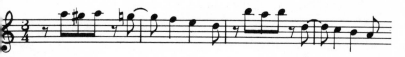

6 measures

6 measures

6 measures

0 measures

A. Berlin: Deutsche Staatsbibliothek, Mus. MS 103
(autograph).

RONDO IN G

Mässig, 44 measures

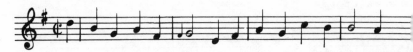

A. Kleine Clavierstücke / nebst / einigen Oden / von /
verschiedenen Tonkünstlern. Two volumes.
Berlin: F. W. Birnstiel, 1760, I, 6-7.

Fantasia

A. Berlin: Deutsche Staatsbibliothek, Mus. MS 103
(autograph).

THEME AND VARIATIONS

Grazioso, 112 measures

A. "Clavier Varizon / von / C. Nichelmann."
Berlin: Deutsche Staatsbibliothek, Mus. MS 103
(autograph).

The variations were at one time catalogued in Berlin as Mus. MS 16168.

WORKS FOR INSTRUMENTAL ENSEMBLE

WORKS FOR INSTRUMENTAL ENSEMBLE

UVERTURE IN B-FLAT

empo lacking, 138 measures

ouree I, 24 measures

rio, 28 measures

enuet I, 24 measures

enuet II, 24 measures

igue, 48 measures

A. "Ouverture B dur / per / due Violini / due Oboi / Viola /
    Basso continue / Partitur / di Nichelmann / 1737."
    Berlin: Deutsche Staatsbibliothek, M. Th. 173, score
    (autograph).

SINFONIA IN F MAJOR

Allegro, 121 measures

Andante, tutti piano, 25 measures

Presto, 94 measures

A. "Sinfonia a F. / a 4 / Violino Primo / Violino Secondo
/ Viola / e / Basso / di Nichelman."
London: British Museum, Add. MS 32171, four
part-books.

SINFONIA IN G MAJOR

Allegro, 64 measures

Adagio, 41 measures

Presto, 102 measures

A. "Sinfonia / a / Violino 1. / Violino 2. / Viola / e / Basso / del / Sig. Nichelmann."
London: British Museum, Add. MS 32171, four part-books.

INFONIA from the SERENATA, IL SOGNO DI SCIPIONE

llegro con brio, 104 measures

ndante, 44 measures

resto, 71 measures

A. "Serenata / Il sogno / di / Scipione / Drammatico Componimento / da Rappresentarsi / Nel Regio Teatro di Berlino / per ordine / Di Sua Maesta / del Nichelman / (Text von Metastasio)."
Rostock: Universitätsbibliothek Rostock, Mus. saec. XVIII, 49^3, score.

B. "Sinfonia a 10."
Schwerin: Mecklenburgische Landesbibliothek, Sig. mus. 4030, ten part-books.

The instrumental sinfonia preceding Il sogno di Scipione is listed as a separate instrumental work as it was copied and later published separately. Also, six arias from Il sogno were arranged by an unknown scribe and are listed as the following six Orchesterstücke.

SIX ORCHESTERSTÜCKE from IL SOGNO DI SCIPIONE

From "Fra la procelle": aria -- Constanza
Allegro, 201 measures

From "Se vuoi che te raccolgano": aria -- Publio
Andante, 123 measures

From "Quercia annosa": aria -- Publio
Allegro, 72 measures

From "Risolver non osa": aria -- Scipione
Allegro, 72 measures

From "Ciglio, che al sol si gira": aria -- Constanza
Allegro, 203 measures

From "So ben nume in costante": aria -- Scipione
Moderato, 244 measures

A. "Orchesterstücke."
    S c h w e r i n :   Mecklenburgische Landesbibliothek, Sig.
    mus. 4031a-c, three part-books.

WORKS FOR VOICE

WORKS FOR VOICE

IL SOGNO DI SCIPIONE: A SERENATA
    In two acts for five solo voices, four-part chorus, two horns,
two oboes, two flutes, two violins, viola, and bass.

ACT I

"Vieni e siegni": recitative -- Fortuna, Constanza, Scipione
Tempo lacking, 53 measures

"Risolver non osa": aria -- Scipione
Allegro, 73 measures

"Guista e la tua richiesta": recitative -- Constanza, Fortuna
Tempo lacking, 13 measures

"Lieve sono al par del vento": aria -- Fortuna
Allegro, 333 measures

"Dunque ove son": recitative -- Scipione, Constanza, Fortuna
Tempo lacking, 41 measures

"Ciglio, che al sol si gira": aria -- Constanza
Allegro, 206 measures

"E quali abitatori": recitative -- Scipione, Fortuna, Constanza
Tempo lacking, 12 measures

"Germe di cento eroi": chorus, horns, and strings
Tempo lacking, 160 measures

"Numi e vero": recitative -- Scipione, Publio
Tempo lacking, 43 measures

"Se vuoi che te raccolgano": aria -- Publio
Andante, 129 measures

ACT II

"Se qui vivon gli eroi": recitative -- Scipione, Fortuna, Constanza, Emilio
Tempo lacking, 75 measures

'Voi collaggiu ridete": aria -- Emilio
Moderato, 72 measures

"Publio, padre, ah lasciate": recitative -- Scipione, Fortuna, Constanza,
  Emilio
Tempo lacking, 35 measures

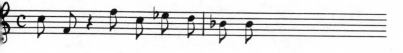

"Quercia annosa": aria -- Publio
Allegro, length unknown, as one page of manuscript is missing, but see
  the third of the preceding Orchesterstücke.

"Giache al voler de fati": recitative -- Scipione, Constanza, Fortuna
Tempo lacking, 38 measures

"A chi seren'io miro": aria -- Fortuna
Allegro, length unknown, as mid-section of the aria is missing

Of the recitative by Scipione, "A si enorme possanza," only
the last fifteen measures of text and music remain.

"Fra la procelle": aria -- Constanza
Allegro, 202 measures

"No piu bella Constanza": recitative -- Scipione
Tempo lacking, 14 measures

"So ben nume in costante": aria -- Scipione
Moderato, 244 measures

"E v'e mortal che ardisca": accompanied recitative -- Fortuna, Scipione
Tempo lacking, 44 measures

"Non paventi giamai le cadute": chorus and full orchestra
Tempo lacking, 1 2 9   m e a s u r e s

A. "Serenata / Il sogno / di / Scipione / Drammatico
Componimento / da Rappresentarsi / Nel Regio Teatro
di Berlino / per ordine / Di Sua Maesta / del Nichelman
/ (Text von Metastasio)."
R o s t o c k :   Universitätsbibliothek Rostock, <u>Mus.</u> <u>saec.</u>
XVIII, 49^3, score.

T e x t :   Pietro Metastasio [Antonio Domenico Bonaventura
Trapassi] (1698-1782)

REQUIEM
Four-part chorus, two flutes, two oboes, two violins, viola, and bass

"Requiem aeternam": chorus and full orchestra
<u>Lento</u>, 1 2 2 m e a s u r e s

"Kyrie eleison": soprano, tenor, oboe, and strings
<u>A d a g i o</u>, 2 0 m e a s u r e s

"Dies irae": bass and strings
Vivace, 13 measures

"Tuba mirum": alto and strings
Vivace, 21 measures

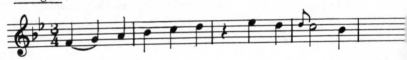

"Recordare": soprano, oboe, and strings
Adagio, 23 measures

"Lacrimosa": chorus and full orchestra
Adagio, 41 measures

"Domine Jesu Christe": chorus and full orchestra
Moderato, 39 measures

"Hostias": chorus and full orchestra
Adagio moderato, 38 measures

"Sanctus": chorus and full orchestra
Poco andante, 54 measures

"Benedictus": alto, flute, violin, and bass
Allegro moderato, 58 measures

"Agnus Dei": chorus and full orchestra
Andante, 74 measures

"Lux aeterna": chorus and strings
Lento, 26 measures

A. "Requiem aternam / componiert / von /
    Nichelmann / (in eigenhandigen Partitur 10 S.)."
    Berlin: Deutsche Staatsbibliothek, Mus. MS N.,
    score (autograph).

CANTATA
High voice, two violins, viola, and bass

"Zeffirretti": aria
Allegro, 163 measures

"Qual dolce rimembranza": accompanied recitative
Adagio, 180 measures

"Giusti dei che in ciel": aria
Adagio, 180 measures

"E per lui ch'oggi": recitative
Tempo lacking, 25 measures

"Quel rapido torrente": aria
Vivace, 267 measures

A.   "Cantata del Sigr. Nichelmann."
Washington: Library of Congress, M 1613 A2N59,
score (autograph).

Text: author unknown

The cantata is the only autograph manuscript of Nichelmann known outside German libraries. The work was contained in an extensive collection of secular vocal music purchased by the Library of Congress from the Leipzig firm of Leo Liepmannssohn on April 2, 1907. Appreciation is expressed to William Lichtenwanger, Music Division, Library of Congress, for his assistance in tracing this manuscript.

The remaining vocal works by Nichelmann, listed in alphabetical order according to the first line of text, were originally published in the format of an open, two-part keyboard score with the text presented below the top part. In works represented by more than one source, the tempo designation of the earliest source, or its absence, is stated in the musical incipit; variants are appended to the appropriate source.

'Ach! kleine Brunette"
Artig und hurtig, 12 measures

A. "Ode," Oden mit Melodien. Two volumes.
    Berlin: F. W. Birnstiel, 1753-1755, I, 20.

B. "Ode," Auserlesene Oden zum Singen beym Clavier, vom Herrn Capellmeister Graun und einigen andern guten Meistern. Two volumes.
    Berlin: Arnold Wever, 1764, II, 16.

C. "An eine Tochter," Lieder der Deutschen mit Melodien. Ed. Christian Gottfried Krause. Four volumes.
    Berlin: George Ludewig Winter, 1767-1768, III, 20.

    Text: Johann Wilhelm Ludwig Gleim (1719-1803)

85

"Bruder, siehst du Rheinwein Blinken" (duet)
Tempo lacking, 30 measures

A. "Das aufgehobene Gebot," Kritische Briefe über die
Tonkunst. Ed. Friedrich W. Marpurg. Three volumes.
Berlin: F. W. Birnstiel, 1760-1764, I, 110-111.

B. "Das aufgehobene Gebot," Kleine Sing- und Spielstücke
furs Clavier von verschiedenen Meistern. Three volumes.
Berlin: F. W. Birnstiel, 1762-1766, III, 6-7.

Text: Gotthold Ephraim Lessing (1729-1781)

"Da hangst du, Jesus"
Tempo lacking, 16 measures

A. "Passionsandacht," Geistliche, moralische und weltliche
Oden von verschiedenen Dichtern und Componisten.
Berlin: Gottl. August Lang, 1758, p. 19.

Text: Samuel Gotthold Lange (1711-1781)

"Das Ende vieler dunkeln Tage"
Traurig, 11 measures

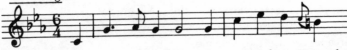

A. "Die Nacht," Berlinische Oden und Lieder. Two volumes.
Leipzig: J. G. I. Breitkopf, 1756-1759, I, 13.

B. "De Nacht," Haerlemse Zangen, In Musicq gesteld by de
Heeren Marpurg, Agricola, Schale, Nichelman, Bach, en
andere vermaarde Componisten.
Haerlem: Izaak en Johannes Enschede, 1761, p. 13.

Text: Friedrich Wilhelm Zachariae (1726-1777)

"Der Hirt, Amint"
Tempo lacking, 22 measures

A. "Amint," Berlinische oden und Lieder. Two volumes.
    Leipzig: J. G. I. Breitkopf, 1756-1759, I, 35.

B. "Amintas," Haerlemse Zangen, In Musicq gesteld by
    de Heeren Marpurg, Agricola, Schale, Nichelman,
    Bach, en andere vermaarde Componisten.
    Haerlem: Izaak en Johannes Enschede, 1761, p. 35.
    Tempo designated as a la Menuette.

    Text: Johann Samuel Patzke (1727-1787)

"Der Mucker rühmet uns das Wasser"
Tempo lacking, 27 measures

A. "Die Unwahrheit," Berlinische Oden und Lieder. Two
    volumes.
    Leipzig: J. G. I. Breitkopf, 1756-1759, II, 11.

    Text: Christian Gottlieb Lieberkühn. According to
    Wilhelm Kosch, Deutsches Literatur-Lexikon (four vol-
    umes; Bern: A. Franke Verlag, 1949-1958), II, 1526, the
    dates of C. G. Lieberkühn are unknown. He was active
    as a poet around the middle of the eighteenth century.

"Der Neid, O Kind"
Lebhaft, 17 measures

"Der Neid, O Kind" (Continued)

A. "Der Neid," Kritische Briefe über die Tonkunst. Ed.
   Friedrich W. Marpurg. Three volumes.
   Berlin: F. W. Birnstiel, 1760-1764, I, 132.

B. "Der Neid," Kleine Sing- und Spielstücke furs Clavier
   von verschiedenen Meistern. Three volumes.
   Berlin: F. W. Birnstiel, 1762-1766, II, 1.

   Text: G. E. Lessing

"Der Welt das Wasser anzupreisen"
Sittsam, 24 measures

A. "Ode," Oden mit Melodien. Two volumes.
   Berlin: F. W. Birnstiel, 1753-1755, I, 11.

B. "Ode," Auserlesene Oden zum Singen beym Clavier,
   vom Herrn Capellmeister Graun und einigen andern
   guten Meistern. Two volumes.
   Berlin: Arnold Wever, 1764, II, 7.

C. "Gränzen der Pflicht," Lieder der Deutschen mit Melodien. Ed. Christian Gottfried, Krause. Four volumes.
   Berlin: George Ludewig Winter, 1767-1768, II, 72.

   Text: Friedrich von Hagedorn (1708-1754)

"Du bist viel gnädiger"
Mässig, 22 measures

A. "Busslied," Geistliche Oden, in Melodien gesetzt von
    einigen Tonkünstlern in Berlin.
    Berlin: C. F. Voss, 1758, p. 3.

    Text: Friedrich Gottlieb Klopstock (1724-1803)

"Ein Freund gelehrter Schulgezanke"
In mässiger Bewegung, 8 measures

A. "Scherzlied," Kritische Briefe über die Tonkunst.
    Ed. Friedrich W. Marpurg. Three volumes.
    Berlin: F. W. Birnstiel, 1760-1764, I, 24.

B. "Scherzlied," Kleine Sing- und Spielstücke furs
    Clavier von verschiedenen Meistern. Three volumes.
    Berlin: F. W. Birnstiel, 1762-1766, III, 9.

    Text: J. W. L. Gleim

"Ein Geist, der sich zu seiner Zeit"
Tempo lacking, 27 measures

A. "Ode," Kleine Klavierstücke nebst einigen Oden von
    verschiedenen Tonkünstlern. Two volumes.
    Berlin: F. W. Birnstiel, 1760, I, 16-17.

    Text: author unknown

"Einsame, angenehme Wüste"
Angenehm, 21 measures

    A. "Ode," <u>Kleine Klavierstücke</u> nebst einigen Oden von
        verschiedenen Tonkünstlern. Two volumes.
        Berlin: F. W. Birnstiel, 1760, I, 15.

        Text: author unknown

"Ergötzt euch, Freunde"
Tempo lacking, 17 measures

    A. "Die Freude," <u>Berlinische Oden und Lieder</u>. Two volumes.
        Leipzig: J. G. I. Breitkopf, 1756-1759, I, 32.

    B. "De Vreuyd," <u>Haerlemse Zangen, In Musicq gesteld by de</u>
        <u>Heeren Marpurg, Agricola, Schale, Nichelman, Bach, en</u>
        <u>andere vermaarde Componisten.</u>
        Haerlem: Izaak en Johannes Enschede, 1761, p. 32.
        Tempo designated as <u>Allegro</u>.

        Text: Johann Peter Uz (1720-1796)

"Falle doch auf Doris Augenlieder"
Tempo lacking, 18 measures

    A. "An den Schlaf," <u>Berlinische Oden und Lieder</u>. Two volumes.
        Leipzig: J. G. I. Breitkopf, 1756-1759, II, 12.

        Text: J. W. L. Gleim

'Gefesselt hang ich an Ismenen"
Tempo lacking, 12 measures

A. "Scherzlied," Kritische Briefe über die Tonkunst.
    Ed. Friedrich W. Marpurg. Three volumes.
    Berlin: F. W. Birnstiel, 1760-1764, I, 126.

B. "Scherzlied," Kleine Sing- und Spielstücke furs Clavier
    von verschiedenen Meistern. Three volumes.
    Berlin: F. W. Birnstiel, 1762-1766, III, 17.

    Text: J. W. L. Gleim

"In einer schwälen Sommerstunde"
Tempo lacking, 24 measures

A. "Scherzlied," Friedrich W. Marpurg, Historisch-krittische
    Beyträge zur Aufnahme der Musik. Five volumes.
    Berlin: Schütz (I) and G. A. Lang (II-V), 1754-1778,
    I, 181.

    Text: author known only as Griess

"Man ist geplagt auf allen Seiten"
Tempo lacking, 22 measures

A. "Der Unwillige," Berlinische Oden und Lieder. Two
    volumes.
    Leipzig: J. G. I. Breitkopf, 1756-1759, I, 3.

"Man ist geplagt auf allen Seiten" (Continued)

B. "De Moei jelyke," Haerlemse Zangen, In Musicq gesteld
by de Heeren Marpurg, Agricola, Schale, Nichelman,
Bach, en andere vermaarde Componisten.
Haerlem: Izaak en Johannes Enschede, 1761, p. 3.
Tempo designated as Temperante.

Text: F. W. Zachariae

"O Mutter, brich die armen Rosen nicht"
Unschuldig, 24 measures

A. "Ode," Oden mit Melodien. Two volumes.
Berlin: F. W. Birnstiel, 1753-1755, I, 27.

B. "Die Mutter und die Tochter," Lieder der Deutschen mit
Melodien. Ed. Christian Gottfried Krause. Four volumes.
Berlin: George Ludewig Winter, 1767-1768, I, 56-57.

Text: author unknown

"Rosen sollen mich bekränzen"
Tempo lacking, 24 measures

A. "Die Vortheile der Jugend," Berlinische Oden und Lieder.
Two volumes.
Leipzig: J. G. I. Breitkopf, 1756-1759, II, 13.

Text: J. P. Uz

Singst du denn nicht einmal wieder" (duet)
empo lacking, 47 measures

A.   "Amor und der Dichter," Kleine Klavierstücke nebst einigen
     Oden von verschiedenen Tonkünstlern. Two volumes.
     Berlin: F. W. Birnstiel, 1760, II, 6-7.

B.   "Amor und der Dichter," Lieder der Deutschen mit Melo-
     dien. Ed. Christian Gottfried Krause. Four volumes.
     Berlin: George Ludewig Winter, 1767-1768, II, 86-88.

     Text: author unknown

So kehre wieder zuruck"
angsam, 23 measures

A.   "Phantasie," Neue Lieder zum Singen beim Clavier.
     Ed. Friedrich W. Marpurg.
     Berlin: G. A. Lang, 1756, pp. 17-18.

     Text: F. W. Zachariae

Voll heilger Lust kennt meine Brust"
ässig, 14 measures

A.   "Die Unsterblichkeit," Geistliche Oden, in Melodien
     gesetzt von einigen Tonkünstlern in Berlin.
     Berlin: C. F. Voss, 1758, p. 26.

     Text: S. G. Lange

Artig und hurtig, 12 measures

A. Deutsche Oden um 1750. No. 108 of Zeitschrift für
Spielmusik auf allerlei Instrumenten.
Celle: Herman Moeck Verlag, 1942, p. 1. Adapted
from "Ach! kleine Brunette."

Sittsam, 24 measures

A. Deutsche Oden um 1750. No. 108 of Zeitschrift für
Spielmusik auf allerlei Instrumenten.
Celle: Herman Moeck Verlag, 1942, p. 7. Adapted
from "Der Welt das Wasser anzupreisen."

PUBLICATIONS OF NICHELMANN'S WORKS

APPEARING AFTER 1800

PUBLICATIONS OF NICHELMANN'S WORKS
APPEARING AFTER 1800

The following publications are listed in alphabetical order by editor.

TTNER, CARL
   Konzert für Cembalo und Streichorchester. No. 145
f Nagels Musik-archiv. Celle: Nagels Verlag, 1938.
   Concerto XIII in A major.
   The figured bass which appeared in the manuscript keyboard part-book
r this concerto is realized in small notes in the upper staff of the keyboard
rt. Metronome indications have been added and diminuendos have been
langed to the horizontal wedges of modern notation.

CKINSON, CLARENCE
   Historical Recital Series for Organ. Two volumes.
ew York: H. W. Gray, 1917-1920.
   Vol. II, No. 22. Claviersuite from the miscella-
eous pieces.

RRENC, JACQUES HIPPOLYTE ARISTEDE, and FARRENC, JEANNE
   Le Trésor des Pianistes. Twenty-three volumes.
ris: L. Farrenc, 1861-1872.
   Vol. X. Sonatas III-VI, XIX, and VIII-XIII.
   This important anthology of keyboard music contains the largest single
llection of Nichelmann's music in a modern publication. It follows the
iginal published texts accurately except for the ornamentation, which
s been altered in varying degrees of consistency. The sonatas are pref-
ed by a brief biographical sketch which is not entirely accurate.

SCHER, HANS, and OBERDÖRFFER, FRITZ
   Deutsche Klaviermusik des 17. und 18. Jahrhunderts.
ine volumes. Berlin: Chr. Friedrich Vieweg, 1937.
   Vol. VIII. Allegro in E-flat, two-four, from the
iscellaneous pieces.
   Vol. IX. Allegro in E major, two-four, from the
iscellaneous pieces.
   This constitutes one of the most accurate editions of Nichelmann's
usic. A second edition appeared in 1960 without the detailed prefaces
the first.

FISCHOF, JOSEPH, and ZELLNER, LEOPOLD ALEXANDER

Klassische Studien für das Pianoforte. Nine volum Vienna: Haslinger, 1866-1869?

Vol. VIII. Sonata IV in G major

The edition was begun by Fischof and completed after his death by Zellner. A reprint by Schlesingerisch Buch and Musikhandlung in Berlin appeared sometime prior to 1910.

FRIEDLAENDER, MAX

Das deutsche Lied im 18. Jahrhundert. Two volum Berlin: J. G. Cotta, 1902; Hildesheim: Georg Olms, 1962 (reprint).

Vol. I, Pt. 2. Lied, "Die Unwahrheit."

GUNTHER, FELIX

Deutsche Tonwerke des 17. und 18. Jahrhunderts, Ser. II of Hausmusik herausgegeben vom Kunstwart. Two volumes. Munich: Kunstwart Verlag, 1907.

Vol. II. Sonata IV in G major.

HERRMANN, KURT

Lehrmeister und Schüler Joh. Seb. Bachs. Two volumes. Leipzig: Hug, 1935.

Vol. II. Presto in E minor from the miscellaneou pieces.

KÖHLER, LOUIS

Les Maîtres du clavecin. Two volumes. Braunschwe Henry Litolff, 1860-1873.

Vol. I. La Gaillarde, La Tendre, Sarabande, and Gigue from the miscellaneous pieces.

KREUTZ, ALFRED

Clavierstücke für Anfänger. Mainz: B. Schott's Söhne, 1937.

Menuets in G major and G minor, Polonaise in A major.

MAXIM, GEORGE PRATT

Masters of the Claviers. New York: Carl Fischer, 1928.

Sarabande from the miscellaneous pieces.

The Sarabande has been excerpted from the Claviersuite and transposed from C minor to B minor.

NIEMANN, WALTER

Old Masters of the 16th, 17th, and 18th Centuries. New York: Edwin F. Kalmus, n.d.

La Gaillarde, La Tendre, Sarabande, Gigue, and Sonata in E-flat (one movement) from the miscellaneous pieces.

The Sonata is the Allegretto in E-flat, three-eight meter, which originally appeared in Marpurg's Clavierstücke. The Kalmus edition is an exact reprint of the Alte Meister des Clavierspiels, originally published at Leipzig by C. F. Peters, n.d.

PAUER, ERNST

Alte Claviermusik in chronologische Folge. Two series of six volumes each. Leipzig: Senff, 1860-1867.

Ser. II, Vol. III. La Gaillarde, La Tendre, Sarabande, and Gigue from the miscellaneous pieces.

PRESS, MICHAEL

Stücke alter Meister für Violine und Clavier bearbeitet. Leipzig: Breitkopf & Härtel, n.d.

Sarabande and Gigue from the miscellaneous pieces.

RICHTER-HAASER, HANS

Variationen und Fugue über ein Thema von Nichelmanns, op. 20. Augsburg: Zientner, 1935.

The variations are based on the Sarabande from the miscellaneous pieces.

SCHNEIDER, MAX
Sinfonie in Es dur. Vol. IV of Mittel- und Nord-
deutsche Kammersinfonien. Nine volumes. Leipzig:
Breitkopf & Härtel, 195-.
Sinfonia to Il sogno di Scipione.
The catalogue of the Bibliothèque nationale gives 1954 as the pub-
lication date; the Riemann Musik Lexikon, ed. Wilibald Gurlitt (3 vols.;
12th ed.; Mainz: B. Schott's Söhne, 1959-1961), II, 311, states 1956.
The edition includes a realized continuo part, although none is indicated
in the autograph manuscript.

SCHROEDER (SCHRÖDER), KARL
Fünf klassische Stücke älterer berühmter Meister
für Violoncell und Pianoforte Eingerichtet. Leipzig:
Breitkopf & Härtel, 188-.
Sarabande from the miscellaneous pieces.

The works listed below are known to contain the
works of Nichelmann designated, but copies of these
publications have not received critical examination.

ABERT, W.
Neue Musik-Zeitung, XXIV (1913).
Sonata in E-flat major.

ESSNER, WALTHER
Berühmte Tanzweisen alter Meister für Violine und
Pianoforte.
La Gaillarde from the miscellaneous pieces.